100 + Top Tips

For

Managing your Coaching Needs

Written by the Healthskills Team of Mark Greenfield, Dawn Scott, Mike Nelson, Ian Munro, Bob Baker, Melanie Warner, Vicky Glanville

Copyright 2018

Published by Ian S Munro

Licence and Copyright Notes

All rights reserved. No part of this book may be reproduced or transmitted in any form or by any means, electronic or mechanical, including photocopying, recording, or by an information storage and retrieval system -- except by a reviewer who may quote brief passages in a review to be printed in a magazine, newspaper, or on the web -- without permission in writing from the publisher Ian S Munro

Front and rear cover design - by Deborah Wood

Proof reading by Tess Knight of Healthskills Ltd

Printed in the United Kingdom by Printondemand-worldwide.com

A CPI catalogue record for this book is available from the British Library.

ISBN: 978-0-9934658-7-1

The publisher has taken every precaution to ensure that the information contained in this book is accurate and complete.

While all attempts have been made to verify information provided in this publication, the publisher and the authors assume no responsibility for errors, omissions, or contrary interpretation of the subject matter herein. Any perceived slights of specific persons, peoples, or organisations are purely unintentional.

By reading this book, the reader agrees that under no circumstances are the publisher and/or authors responsible for any losses (direct or indirect) that are incurred as a result of using the information contained including - but not limited to errors, omissions, or inaccuracies.

The legal entity for Ian S Munro is NextStepsGroup Ltd, registered office: 2 Crossways Business Centre, Kingswood, Aylesbury, HP18 0RA, UK

COPYRIGHT OF OTHER AUTHORS:

In this book we the authors and publisher make reference to the work of other authors. We acknowledge the copyright of these authors. We are not attempting to pass off their work as ours. We hope that by mentioning them in this book this will help to promote their work to a wider audience.

With thanks to

Healthskills Group Limited

The Healthskills Group is a leading provider of Leadership, Team and Organisational Development programmes and a range of related services to the Public, Private and Voluntary sectors, supporting clients to improve and sustain their Organisational Health.

Their programmes are delivered across all levels of organisations and they receive constant accolades from those who participate in their programmes.

The authors either work directly or as Partners or Advisors. They all operate to the ethical and regulatory standards of either; The European Mentoring and Coaching Council; The International Coaching Federation or The Association for Coaching.

They coach across all levels from supervisor levels to boards meaning they have comprehensive knowledge of today's changing workplace.

All the authors are delighted to be associated and wish Healthskills continued good health!

info@healthskills.co.uk

Books in this series

BLUE BOOKS FOR PERSONAL DEVELOPMENT

100 + TOP TIPS FOR JOB SEEKERS
ISBN 978-095700-853-3

100 + TOP TIPS FOR DEVELOPING YOUR CAREER
ISBN 978-095700-858-8

100 + TOP TIPS FOR EFFECIVE LEADERSHIP
ISBN 978-0-9934658-6-4

100 + TOP TIPS FOR MANAGING YOUR COACHING NEEDS
ISBN 978-0-9934658-7-1

RED BOOKS FOR IMPROVING YOUR ORGANISATION – SMALL AND LARGE

100 + TOP TIPS FOR SETTING UP AND RUNNING AN ONLINE BUSINESS
ISBN 978-099346-580-2

100 + TOP TIPS FOR EFFECTIVE SALES MANAGEMENT
ISBN 978-095700-859-5

100 + TOP TIPS FOR EFFECTIVELY USING ONLINE SOCIAL MEDIA
ISBN 978-099346-582-6

100 + TOP TIPS FOR SETTING UP YOUR OWN BUSINESS
ISBN 978-099346-584-0

Books can be purchased in Paperback and some in eBook form too. Visit www.100toptips.com

Introduction

Coaching has become a "must have" in organisations of all size across the world. Coaching is recognised as a major contributor in the development of new and existing leaders. It is also used as a means of supporting managers whose performance has slipped and is a recognised means of giving them the support to get back on track.

Coaching can be delivered on a 1:1, group, or team basis.

Many books have been written about Coaching ranging from explanations about how coaching works, different types of coaching, how to become a coach and different coaching scenarios.

To people, on the surface, coaching looks complicated and many do not really understand how it is meant to work. It is often unclear how a coaching programme can lead to improvement in the person being coached with obvious advantages to their organisation.

As a group of practising coaches, we have written this book to explode a number of the myths around coaching and to give the reader straight forward commentary and advice about what coaching is and how it works.

The purpose of this book is to address the needs of 3 different groups of people:

1. Those who are about to go on a coaching programme and what steps can they take to get the most out of their coaching relationship.
    This is covered in Part 1
2. Those who have been on a coaching programme and who would like to incorporate coaching techniques into their team and/or peer management group.
    This is covered in Part 2.
3. Those whose role is to procure coaching services for their organisation and some helpful tips about how to procure the best coaches for their purpose.
    This covered in Part 3.

Having read the part of the book that most relates to the reader's needs, our advice is that the whole book should be read. By doing this the reader will get a clearer understanding about the wider issues of coaching.

Because we are addressing the needs of three different sets of people, you will occasionally read something in one part of the book that was also mentioned in another part of the book. This is unavoidable as some people will initially only reads their part of the book.

A few words about the Learning Zone. Some of the chapters have forms for the reader which are explained in greater depth and illustrated in The Learning Zone. So that the reader can download blank forms to use on these exercises, all they have to do is go to our book site http://100toptips.com register as a user – your privacy is our priority – and you can download the forms from the Learning Zone on the site for your own use.

Hoping you enjoy the book and please let us have any comments at feedback.coaching@100toptips.com

THE AUTHORS

Mark Greenfield   Ian Munro   Bob Baker   Vicky Glanville

Dawn Scott   Mike Nelson   Melanie Warner

Contents

Chapter 1

Top 10 Tips for Understanding the difference between Mentoring, Coaching and Moaching

By Ian Munro

At the start of our book, we thought it might be helpful to take a light-hearted look at the differences between these three areas; coaching, mentoring and moaching.

Our experience is that organisations often confuse mentoring with coaching and vice versus. Hopefully this will clear such matters up although the addition of moaching is not intended to confuse.

1.   The benefits of Mentoring

Mentoring is often provided by a more senior person than the "mentee". The benefit is that mentors bring a depth and breadth of knowledge and expertise of the organisation.

- The mentor often comes from a related part of the organisation but often not from within the same unit. This means they may have a different view on an issue than your team.
- Mentoring relationships tend to be for a longer period than coaching. The benefit is that a stronger relationship can be developed.
- Mentors often offer solutions to the challenges you have.
- Outcomes will not necessarily have been developed by you – so who owns the solution?

2.   The downsides of Mentoring

- Mentor sessions tend to have to be booked several weeks ahead meaning that mentors are not always available at short notice. The mentee may not wish to share some of their deeper concerns with the Mentor as they are involved within the organisation.

- This means that some deeper issues may not be resolved leading to a potential longer-term problem for the organisation and the mentee.
- Time pressures on the Mentor can lead to shallow discussions and contributions.
- The Mentor may not have been trained as a mentor, nor had continual professional development.

3.   The benefits of coaching

- Coaches will work with you to help you create the solutions to your challenges.
- Coaches bring a wider range of other organisation environments to the coaching discussion.
- Coaches are totally independent from the sponsoring organisation – unless employed as internal coaches.
- Coaches should have current accreditation with their professional body, be supervised as coaches and have ongoing ethical training.
- Coaching programmes are goal focused for the coaching period with three-way assessments and at the beginning and end with the sponsor.
- Coaching programmes can last from three months to over twelve months – with defined goals.
- Outcomes will be developed by you.

4.   The downsides of Coaching

- Coaches are not potentially available instantly as they will mainly be working in other organisations.
- Coaches will not be over familiar with the organisations culture.
- Coachees can be guaranteed confidentiality.

However, coachees need to be aware that this is on the proviso that you are doing nothing to harm the organisation or ethically the coach will have to disclose this information.

5. What does this tell you?

- You need to define whether you need a Mentor or Coach. Talk this through with line management and Talent Management within your organisation.
- Are your objectives/goals short term 6-9 months or 12-18 months?
- Will the results need to be delivered in a tight time window in which case coaching may be the best option for you?

6. The benefits of Moaching

- Moaching is not a word you will have seen in Coaching and Mentoring publications. However, from a pragmatic point in delivering a coaching session it can lead the coachee to possible solutions more quickly.
- Moaching works as a blend of mentoring and coaching particularly when you are time pressed and need to see some options in the short term.
- Coaches Moach but mentors do not.
- You will be able to fast track three to four options to your challenge if your coach operates as a Moach.
- It is likely at the next session that it will be purely coaching as the coach probes your rationale and reasoning for the options of your choice.

7.   The downsides of Moaching

- Only a short-term measure to help you resolve a short-term issue by the coach pointing you at two or three solutions.
- It is not part of the longer-term coach goal setting.
- Do not use it too often. For coaching to be beneficial you have to be prepared to allocate adequate time before and after each session.

8.   Blending all three

- There are many coaching situations where time needs to be taken out to look at different approaches.
- Initially some coaches will use Moaching to fast track progress where time is short at the start of a new goal.
- Giving pointers to a coachee to kick start a process is fine. Essentially, they have to own the outputs and plan and manage the next steps.

9.   Options going forward

- If you have a key area that needs resolution or you need to kick start the resolution process, discuss Moaching with your coach.
- Do not be surprised if they suggest it.
- Better planning for your coaching programme reduces the need for short term solutions.
- However, we all know that organisations can throw us challenges that come out of the blue.
- Review carefully whether you need a mentor or coach or both.

10. Making it work for you

- Your coach should be working with your sponsor and you on anticipated goals and outcomes from your programme.
- Invest adequate time to plan for this – your organisation is investing in you.
- The organisation may have guidelines for Mentors. Obtain a copy and satisfy yourself whether or not this is your best route.

YOUR NOTES FROM CHAPTER 1

Part 1

How to get the most out of your coaching relationship

Chapter 2

Top 10 Tips for clearly identifying what you and your sponsor want to get out of the process

By Vicky Glanville

This chapter focuses on helping you make the most of your coaching process by keeping your coaching sponsor or line manager firmly in the loop.

By keeping them involved you are more likely to get the support and encouragement you need to ensure that your coaching is successful.

This also keeps you accountable and will help you to share your successes and challenges to support your learning and development.

This section discusses the goal setting process and when to share status updates with your line manager. It talks about personal marketing, asking for ongoing feedback from your peers and ultimately what happens at the end of the process.

1. Initial discussions with Talent Management, your sponsor on required goals and outcomes

- An employer may show that they value you as an employee by giving you the fantastic opportunity of being coached. But it does stand to reason that they will expect to see improvement, change or development in a skill or knowledge area in return.
- For the coaching to be successful, at both a personal and business level, these expectations need to be clearly understood and defined at the outset to ensure an effective conclusion to the coaching process.
- If your manager or sponsor is not involved at this stage and during your coaching process, they will be unable to support your development in a timely manner.

- This can extend from 'greenlighting' time away from the desk to negotiating specific projects to help embed coaching outcomes.
- It's worth noting that coachees who have clear goals defined from their sponsor at the outset have higher levels of satisfaction with their achievements at the end of the coaching process. (Carter and Connage 2007.)
- In the initial session and contracting process, feedback methods, expected timescales, and definition of private and public goals should be agreed.

2. Aligning your goals and outcomes with those of the organisation

- To prevent a disconnect between the organisational goals and your own personal objectives, it makes sense that before you start your coaching process you are clear about the organisations planned trajectory.
- Start with your company's vision, mission and values. Make sure you are aware of the strategic plan so that you are clear about where you fit within it.
- As already stated, during the initial discussions the business goals and outcomes expected as an output from *your* coaching must be clearly defined.
- Your sponsor may state that at least one or two of the defined outcomes must relate to a key business objective so that the coaching has a clear relationship to a known business need. Work with your coach to create measurable metrics so that you can show your organisation the positive steps you are making to meet the organisation goals.

- Prove accountability and communicate your status against the defined outcomes *regularly* to your sponsor or manager.

3.   Creating your Personal Development Plan

- Taking control of my personal development plan has always been the route to increasing my satisfaction and motivation at work. It gave me a sense of ownership and control of my own destiny in the workplace.
- Your PDP establishes your aims and objectives and the action of writing these into a plan makes them more concrete and therefore achievable.
- Use the outputs from your coaching sessions to define your goals, being clear to understand why the goals are important to you.
- Identify areas that you would like to improve on, with a clear plan of action that details how.
- The process forces you to address your strengths and weaknesses, so be honest with yourself!
- Make sure that you define clear measurements so that you can track success.
- Review progress regularly so that you can make sure you are on track. Be flexible and pragmatic as business goals change throughout the year – you may need to adjust your goals in line with these changes.
- You can use your PDP for career progression, developing new skills, career change etc.

4. Sharing likely outputs with your line manager and mentor

- As mentioned earlier, coaching is at its most successful when your line manager or sponsor is fully involved in your coaching process. Three or four way contracting defines at the outset what the critical success factors are and facilitates clear accountability.

- As part of the contracting process, there should be a clear distinction between public goals and private goals. Your private goals are likely to change once your public goals are clearly defined in the initial meeting with your sponsor and the coach.

- The client/coach relationship implies full confidentiality, however the coach is duty bound to escalate issues and disclose information if you reveal that you are in danger of causing serious harm to yourself or someone else; you have been involved in a serious crime; you are contravening your employment contract; or you have raised issues that may affect the protection of a child. All confidentiality clauses should be confirmed at the start of the contract process.

- Levels of transparency and openness should be defined upfront so that everyone is aware what information will be shared publicly and what will be kept private between you and the coach. This extends to private and public goals as well as ongoing feedback.

- Agree timings for sharing outputs at the initial meeting with your line manager and coach. This will depend on the length of the agreed coaching contract but remember that keeping your line manager on board is key to the success of your coaching journey.

5.   Personal Marketing within your organisation

- Coaching's key success factor is proving that coaching interventions work and create change. An effective method of showing this, as stated earlier, is regular feedback on goals. Don't just limit this to your manager or sponsor but share with your peers and managers.
- Self-promotion, unless you are a narcissist, is not an instinctive behaviour in most people and can feel very uncomfortable and unseemly. However, you need to let people know what you are doing, how you've improved, the successes you're having and the obstacles you've overcome. If you focus on facts and don't over embellish you won't come across as bombastic. You have to remember that, in general, the people you work with are not psychic!
- Build and grow your internal networks and seek constructive feedback. This will help you benchmark yourself pre, during and post coaching.
- Get to know your colleagues in your team and in other departments. Seek out opportunities to help, support or encourage them. Don't work in isolation – make sure you are seen and heard.
- Develop your professional scrap book, this is especially useful at appraisal time. Keep information about key projects, successes and points of learning that illustrate your strengths and show a growth mind set. [inserted space]
- Solicit feedback and endorsements from your network. Don't be afraid to ask – most people will feel flattered that you asked their opinion.

6. Getting ongoing feedback from your peer group

- Some organisations undertake 360-degree reviews on a yearly basis but informal feedback from your peers is often the most honest and effective.
- Be brave and ask for blunt and, if need be, brutally honest feedback.
- Don't be vague such as 'how can I improve' or 'do you have any feedback for me,' seek specific answers by providing them with clear questions.
- Tailor your questions to defined themes that align with your coaching and PDP goals. Don't give them an option to provide a yes/no answer.
- Ask in a timely manner – close to an event for example so that they can remember.
- If you don't agree with what they say don't respond immediately to the content. Say thank you and be neutral in your response. You could then review the response in a coaching session if this works from a time perspective. You need to remember that this is their interpretation and they may see things that aren't apparent to you.
- Be careful not to ask for feedback when you feel stressed, angry or anxious as you will struggle to receive any feedback objectively. Wait till you are calm and feeling more positive.
- Don't disregard feedback and if you don't understand their response ask for clarity. But don't do this in a judgemental or patronising manner or they won't respond next time you ask.
- Don't make it too hard to answer, be clear in your questions and only ask for a response about one or two things at a time. Ask for an email response rather than expect them to complete a big form.

- Model great behaviours and make a habit of offering constructive feedback to your peers. Include examples and observations.
- Ultimately you must follow through on feedback – if they have identified a negative behaviour that you concede is true you need to show them you have listened and make changes. If you say thank you and then do nothing, they won't bother providing feedback again.

7. The review points – initial, mid-point, final

- The initial review starts with you undertaking self-assessment around professional goals, reasons for coaching and the type of coaching required.
- The coach will use a range of tools, models and assessments to gather information and understand your values, goals, interests and areas for development. This information will create a baseline from which coaching success can be proven.
- A mid-point assessment will discuss and identify what is working well, what needs to change or improve and whether you are on track with the goals that were identified at the beginning of the process.
- At the completion of the coaching contract, a final assessment will be undertaken to make sure that you reached your goals – for both you and the organisation.
- The coach will want to understand your views of the process, their ability and the effectiveness of the coaching relationship.
- Your baseline assessments will be revisited so that you, the coach and your sponsor/manager can see how you have moved things forward.

- In addition, the coach will want to understand your ongoing commitment to follow through on what has been agreed.
- Your coach may also follow up with you after 6 months, or at another agreed time, to review ongoing process and check in with your baseline assessments.

8.   Dealing with challenges and issues

- You may find that the coaching process brings out issues and challenges you in ways you were not expecting.
- It may force you to be honest with yourself which may be uncomfortable. A good coach will be able to help you navigate through this.
- Remember the coach is there to support you and help you on your development journey. They are there to challenge you to think and act differently – to move you out of your comfort zone. Coaches are looking for that 'light-bulb' moment.
- As you change and evolve through your coaching process, these changes will become apparent to others – for example, your manager and colleagues. This could in turn create other challenges such as blocking and removal of support which is discussed in the next section.
- Use your coaching sessions to discuss and evaluate these challenges and issues – are they real or assumed? Are they positive or negative?
- Coaching is designed to bring about change which can create challenge and conflict. Ultimately it all leads to growth. It depends on your mind set.

9.   Non-supportive colleagues

- It can be a hugely frustrating experience to face colleagues who are not willing to support your coaching outcomes or goals. The key is to understand their reasons why.
- Talk to your coach to gain advice and guidance on how to manage this and use some of their questioning approaches to ascertain more information from the colleague in question.
- Do you instinctively know the reasons why they are not supportive? Take some time to examine each possible reason and plan your response.
- Arrange a meeting with the person. Talk to them – use open ended questions to clearly find out what the issues are.
- If more than one person is being non-supportive – speak to them individually as there may be a strong personality who is influencing the group.
- Listen to hear and don't be defensive or judgemental when speaking to the colleague. They may have a good reason, at least in their eyes, why they won't support you. They may be jealous or frustrated that they haven't been selected for coaching support.
- Model the behaviours you want to see and be surrounded by. Rise above it and treat them the way you want to be treated.
- Focus your efforts on those colleagues who are supporting you and help them in return. Show the non-supportive colleague that it's a win-win situation.
- Keep lines of communication open and don't shut yourself off from them – they might just be having a bad day/week/month.

10.   Final outcomes

- Hopefully you will finish your coaching with a sense of progress, fulfilment and a clear understanding of how you have changed.
- But, as much as you will enjoy your coaching process it will need to end. Effective coaches will plan for this at the beginning so that everyone understands the goal. Ultimately to 'begin with the end in mind'.
- Your coach will help you identify what you can put in place to make sure that your learning and development continues after the coaching ends – this could be in the form of specific training, internal mentoring or books to read.
- You will need to identify with your coach clear goals and direction for moving forward so that you can keep your momentum up. Your contract may also allow for a 'coaching catch-up' within a defined period so that you can both 'check-in' to monitor your ongoing progress.

YOUR NOTES FROM CHAPTER 2

Chapter 3

Top 10 Tips for Effective Chemistry Meetings

By Bob Baker

This chapter provides sections that seek to aid successful chemistry meetings. However, some attention is given to whether to have them and how to structure a relationship if you don't.

Chemistry meetings are designed to determine how the coach and coachee will relate to each other as individuals and problem-solving partners, working together to help the coachee succeed in achieving business, personal development and career objectives.

These initial discussions between coach and coachee to see if there is a "fit" are often seen as a vital part of ensuring:
a) that a coachee feels that they can work with a particular individual.
b) that there is a likely return on investment for an organisation sponsoring coaching.
c) that the coach is comfortable that their style will be effective with the coachee's requirements.

However, whilst the benefits of a chemistry meeting may appear self-evident, they can add to initial cost, become a "beauty parade" from which a coach is chosen and evidence about their effectiveness in aiding successful coaching outcomes appears limited.

Note: The importance of Chemistry meetings detailed in this Chapter are also mentioned in the next chapter in Top Tip 4.

1.   Understand what is "chemistry"

- If a chemistry conversation is an opportunity for the coachee and one (or more) potential coaches to speak with each other - what are they doing it for?

- The notion of "chemistry" implies the sharing of a connection of some sort and a wish to see the other person again. It is slightly nebulous and - in coaching terms - benefits from closer definition.
- Chemistry in coaching concerns personal introductions, understanding background, how the coach will work, past experiences of coaching from the coachee and some discussion about the coaching assignment in terms of what to focus upon and what is hoped to be achieved. Both should leave with an understanding (subjective as it may be) about whether this relationship could work.

2.   How do I know it is there?

- Since "chemistry" is a slightly nebulous concept, what judgements am I likely to make about whether it is there?
- Firstly, beware of unconscious bias – making automatic judgements based upon our background, cultural environment and personal experiences. This may lead a coachee to seek similar or same levels of experience, intellectual capacity, and backgrounds in a coach rather than someone who may bring different styles and thinking and more challenge.
- If you believe that coaching is much less about coach experience in a particular sector that matches the coachee and more about the approach, values and style of the coach then as a coachee you will be looking for someone you can work with and (if your requirements demand it) will not give you an easy ride.

- Lastly, beware of excellent rapport in a chemistry meeting blinding you to potential difficulties or incompatibility further down the line in your coaching relationship. Feeling comfortable and harmonious in a chemistry meeting may be exactly what – as a coachee – you DON'T need!

3.   Face-to-face, phone or skype?

- Technology can be a wonderful tool and provides the opportunity to vary how chemistry meetings can be held.
- If we rule out email (a "blunt instrument" in terms of understanding connections on anything but an information passing level) then the main channels are face-to-face, phone or skype.
- Face-to-face is best because it provides an opportunity to understand what being in the room together will feel like. There is an opportunity to let a conversation flow and to observe and understand the nuances of a relationship. But it can be expensive and time-consuming (particularly if there are a choice of coaches on offer).
- Skype is useful when the distances to travel may be long and may work very well in allowing a helpful conversation with most of the benefits of face-to face.
- Phone conversations are also useful to initiate conversations but limited in terms of the deeper view of chemistry – that slightly intangible feeling that "this relationship will work".

4. Structuring a chemistry meeting 1 (Coach)

- Work out what you want to say and the key themes you want to get across about your coaching, your style and way of working.
- Be flexible in your structure accommodating the needs of your client but ensuring you get all the information you require from them while getting your points across.
- Be ready with client issues that you have worked with and how you jointly with the coachee tackled them. In particular – how did your client benefit.

5. Structuring a chemistry meeting 2 (Coachee)

- Be clear about what attributes of a coach are important to you – this will focus your view of chemistry.
- Be clear about what you want to achieve by the end of the coaching experience – be better at, resolved a problem, applied for a number of appropriate higher-level roles etc.
- Ask for the coach's experience of working with a coachee with similar requirements.
- Discuss what style and approach by the coach may be best for you but be prepared to listen and to be flexible, the coach may have other views which could also be helpful to you.

6. Rapport v Chemistry

- If **rapport** is about a close and harmonious relationship, then **chemistry** implies a more complex interaction between people – understanding and a desire to carry on a relationship yes but not necessarily easy or without challenge.
- It is easy to get seduced by the development of rapport (see section 2 above) but an easy flow in a coaching setting may mean that the difficult questions for the coachee are not being asked. Sometimes a difficult silence is important!
- So coachee - look for a connection and an understanding of what a particular coach might bring. Don't look for harmony and easy conversations.

7. What do I do if it is not there? (Coachee)

- Analyse why it is not there – what is not working? Something you heard when the coach described their experience? The way that they expressed things? A lack of "track record" with similar issues to you own? Just be sure it has some basis.
- What do you want to do about it? You could work at it but maybe you believe that the absence of chemistry is too serious.
- In coaching there is often discussion about "no fault divorces" and here a clean (and early) break may be the best approach.
- If is not as clear cut as it is there or not but rather you have doubts about a couple of aspects then honesty may be the best policy.

- How a coach responds to doubts and questions will say a lot about them and may allay some of your concerns.

8. Finding your "stance" in chemistry meetings

- John Whittington a coach and facilitator (http://www.johnwhittington.com) asserts that good chemistry is about the way a coach thinks about a relationship with the coachee. He argues that using ideas captured in an acronym STANCE will "affirm your approach and enrich the chemistry check experience"
- Details of all the ideas are found at http://thechemistrycheck.com but we have highlighted 3 below.
- **Start at the End** stresses an important question is what the coachee would like the coaching to achieve – what a good outcome would be. This often relieves the anxiety of "where shall we start?"
- **Take in the Whole** asks the question of where the coachee sees themselves in the organisational or cross-organisational system. It pushes for a sense of their place rather than a mark on an organisational chart.
- **Not about You** reminds the coach that the chemistry meeting is not an opportunity to wave qualifications in front of your coachee or prospective coachee. The coachee may ask about qualifications and it would then be strange not to answer but they are more likely to want to want to understand your effectiveness and abilities.

9. Understanding different viewpoints

- The benefits of chemistry meetings for all parties may appear obvious – not least that having them may avoid a costly "mis-match" where the expected outcomes are not forthcoming.
- Erik De Haan strikes a different note however stating that *"the strongest active ingredient is......the agreement that coach and coachee are able to reach on goals and tasks."*
- De Haan also states that *"...personality factors and the match between personality factors of coach and coachee appear to be much less important with little effect on....the general effectiveness of coaching."*
- I have also seen views that fundamentally disagree with chemistry meetings on the basis that
  - a) they lead to prejudice with clients/coachees discriminating against coaches based on their age, gender, ethnicity or indeed any other dimension of difference
  - b) prospective coachees are not always knowledgeable enough about coaching to be able to assess a coach's ability to work with them
  - c) an experienced coach can work with anyone!
- You may agree or disagree with any or all of the points and in section 10 I give my perspective to steer you through the different viewpoints.

10. To have or have not

- So, there are different viewpoints on the value of chemistry meetings – to have them or not to have them?

- Notwithstanding the points raised in section 9, I lean towards holding chemistry meetings as:
  - a) a vehicle for getting important "coaching business" done
  - b) forming a view of the relationship going forward. This is likely to be useful even if the impact on coaching outcomes are limited
- Preparation on both sides will lead to a meeting with purpose. Particularly important is the coachee having a view (or being helped to develop one) on the purpose/end point for coaching. What needs to be different, achieved, changed?
- Being aware of prejudice and bias in who should coach you/who should you coach will also help. Don't use chemistry meetings to confirm your bias – use them to explore possibilities and difference!

YOUR NOTES FROM CHAPTER 3

Chapter 4

Top 10 Tips for Checking and reviewing as your programme unfolds

By Mike Nelson

There are many coaching conversations and programmes which can literally drift along, with little attention paid to the progress of the coachee, the progress of the work or its value to the coachee and/or any potential sponsor, be it organisation or simply the 'paymaster'.

This chapter is designed to raise awareness on thinking on how to keep track of your coaching, and to encourage you to apply a degree of 'Course Correction' if, as a result of your reviewing/evaluating your progress feel that things are not progressing as you may have expected.

1.   Self-Awareness

- Your coach and the coaching process are very likely to increase your sense of self-awareness. Questions like "What am I thinking about that? What am I feeling about that? Why am I thinking/feeling this way?" These and other reflective questions either asked by the coach or by you of yourself will make you more self-aware.
- Self-awareness is useful because it allows us to be more in control of how we go about things and how we might refine/improve these ways of thinking or doing. The coach may use (typically) a 10-point scale (e.g. How do you feel about that situation on a 10-point scale where 1 is the worst possible and 10 is the best possible feeling?) This could give you something to aim for or used in a review as the coaching programme proceeds.
- In time your sense of self-awareness should be developed to the point where it becomes a useful tool to manage yourself, not only in coaching but as you go about your life and work in general.

2.   Goals

- Many coaching programmes will be accompanied by a set of goals, developed by yourself or in conjunction with your coach and/or organisation. Goal setting in this way, providing you feel you 'own' the goals, can provide a useful map and benchmark to aim for in the coaching programme.
- Goals may be set along the lines of S.M.A.R.T. objectives (Specific – Measurable – Achievable – Relevant – Time bound) or may be less structured as one or more statements of intent or aim for your coaching.
- There is a school of thought amongst some coaching practitioners that goals can 'get in the way' of what might be described as 'emergent' coaching (in other words allowing a dialogue to 'flow', guided by coaching questions and your reflections) so that you may get to work on more hidden issues. In this case, some reflective notes made by you after each session or period of reflection could well be useful to help you monitor progress.

3.   Motivation

- Having the motivation to take part in coaching and to feel like you want to work on improving your strengths or development needs is a critical part of the coaching process but also is useful to help you monitor progress.
- Ask yourself how motivated you feel about this work, who is driving this, how different could it be if you changed things – improving skills, knowledge or attitudes to a challenge.

- Some coaches may help you develop a vison of what it could look and feel like if things were different and the very vison itself proving to be a more motivating and measurable outcome which you can work towards.
- If the motivation to do this work is (properly) coming from you then the sense of motivation will help you measure your progress as various goals or landmarks are achieved. Whilst harder to measure in a very objective way a coaching programme that makes you feel better can be as effective (or even more effective) than more tangible results.

4.   Contracting with your Coach

- Most professionally trained coaches will develop a contract with you either before (perhaps in a 'chemistry meeting as described in chapter 3 in this book) or during an initial session. This contract is essential so that you and your coach both know how the coaching will work, the boundaries and how to manage all of these. As a minimum, the contract should include when/where/how often/how long your coaching sessions will be. Also included will be a framework for how the coaching will operate and the rules of confidentiality and boundary management. In this way you will have a practical set of measures around which progress can be monitored.
- Some coaches will provide a more formal written contract whilst others may make this an open discussion between you. In the latter case it would be useful to have a written summary of the things agreed to enable the programme to be monitored.

- It is worth reviewing how this initial contract is operating, either at the end of each session or more commonly approximately halfway through a programme allowing for adjustment to the way the coaching is operating for you.

5. Rapport and Honesty

- Effective coaching takes place in an atmosphere of openness and honesty with a higher level of rapport between you and your coach than you might get in other relationships. It is only in this way that your coach can really help you. As I have told many a line manager "We can't work on things we don't know about".
- One useful measure therefore (although may be hard to define) is how open are you being – open with yourself (relate back to self-awareness) and open with your coach. Of course, this will only operate if there is a sense of trust between you and the coach, but I would suggest that any doubt about trust/rapport/honesty between you and the coach should be discussed if either party feels there is an issue or barrier.
- Remember that developing trust takes time so it may take more than one session for you to feel you can be really open so monitored how open you are feeling will be a useful indicator to effective progress in your coaching programme.

6. Psychometrics/360 Feedback

- Many organisations and some coaches will suggest the use of a 360-degree feedback process to define both a starting point and repeated at a later date to be able to monitor progress.

- This is progress as perceived by others within the organisation. Whether it is conducted informally (by an email survey for example) or more formally using one of the many excellent 360 instruments available this can be an invaluable way of measuring your progress beyond your own perception.

- The use of a psychometric instrument or questionnaire may be recommended by the coach or organisation. There is a myriad of these (PRISM, OPQ, Myers-Briggs Type Indicator etc.) so the choice should be guided by professionals.

- Finally, the most comprehensive (but perhaps the most daunting for some) would be the combination of 360 and one or more psychometrics into a full assessment report which would provide a very robust benchmark against which to set coaching goals and measure progress. In larger organisations these more challenging processes may be mandatory steps to the higher levels of leadership or senior roles.

7.   Feedback

- Without feedback how can you know? At the start of this chapter I opened with the concept of self-awareness and whilst this is invaluable to growth and change it can be limited if we don't compare our perceptions of self with those of others in the world around us.

- Collecting feedback is therefore a valuable tool in being able to benchmark where we are as well as to chart progress.

- There are a variety of feedback frameworks around using mnemonics or frameworks (such as 'BOOST' – Balanced – Observed – Objective – Specific – Timely) or a simple what I should STOP/START/CONTINUE doing set of questions.
- Take time to collate, reflect and think about the feedback. You don't have to 'swallow' it all... which is the feedback that resonates and why is that. If there is a lot of feedback which are the highest priorities, or which is the most frequent from your observers. Remember to collect feedback on your strengths as well as development areas. It can be more effective to build upon strengths that constantly work on development needs.

8.   Evaluation

- Having spent quite a lot of this chapter looking at setting measures, benchmarks and how to gather data for this how would we use this in evaluating the work?
- One very useful framework is that developed by Kirkpatrick – this suggests 4 levels at which evaluation can take place. From level 1 which is about your immediate reaction to the coaching – usually during or at the end of a single session.
- What has struck you and what has emerged from the session – what will you do next? This model progress up to level 4 in which the impact of your coaching has had on the world around you over the whole programme... what has been the benefit to you and the organisation around you.

- Whether you or the coach utilises Kirkpatrick or one of the other systems of evaluation I would suggest this is one of the most useful ingrained habits to develop as a result of the investment of your time into coaching – coupled with self-awareness it can mature into 'self-coaching' in which you can challenge yourself on an ongoing basis for growth and improvement.

9. Running out of Steam!

- This chapter would not be complete without this section. You may feel (or your coach may feel) that you have run out of steam with the coaching. A dip in energy levels or motivation towards the coaching may well be a symptom you recognise. Or any of the methods you may have adopted earlier in this chapter may be showing a lack of progress towards a goal.

- Firstly, ask if the initial goal/aim and/or vison is still relevant (or indeed if it was right in the first place!) Take time to explore what you are thinking or feeling and prepare to discuss this openly with your coach. The coach will find this useful to take a step back with you and check to see if the programme, the style or even if the coach is still right for you. It may just be that with this step back you and the coach can decide on a change of direction or renewing the goals or style/process of coaching. Many coaches will relish this challenge with you and it and could be a real breakthrough to do this if you are stuck. The coach may also raise this if they are feeling out of steam even if you haven't noticed it.

- Do not be concerned about stopping the coaching or changing the coach if, on discussion, this feels appropriate.

10. Sustaining Change

- Stephen Covey (in the book 7 Habits of Highly Effective People) describes the 7th habit as "Sharpening the Saw." In this way he is pointing out the need to stop and reflect before pressing on. Having invested time and energy with your coach and if you review along the way then developing a habit of sharpening the saw can be very useful. Even after the coaching is finished this habit can help you sustain new behaviours and habits moving forward. Practising new skills and embedding them can ensure you are able to really sustain the changes you were seeking – if you measure progress as you go (the whole purpose of this chapter) it should be relatively easy to keep this momentum after the coaching has finished.
- From time to time it may be useful to meet with the original or a new coach to refresh – keeping a record of your progress during the programme can really help this be picked up easily at a future point.
- On a final note – good luck with progress – coaching when it works well is highly rewarding both for the client and the coach. Keeping a track of progress will really help recognise the valuable return on all this investment.

YOUR NOTES FROM CHAPTER 4

Part 2

How to incorporate coaching techniques into your work

Chapter 5

Top 10 Tips for Identifying what you would like to bring to your management style

By Melanie Warner

As a leader and manager, it is your role to ensure the team delivers the results it sets out to and your people are happy. A happy team is likely to be a more productive one. So how do you ensure as a manager, you are being your best self and are fulfilled in your role?

This chapter focuses on a number of key areas for you to consider when exploring your own management style and how you can be authentic in your role whilst leading others to achieve results.

1. Be aware of the impact of your role as a leader and manager

- One of the most cited reasons for individuals leaving their jobs is the culture and work environment. Organisational climate is people's perception of "what it's like to work here?" Where this is perceived to be positive it means individuals are likely to go the extra mile and be your star performers. Whilst there are various factors that impact climate, leadership style is believed to have the biggest impact (50-70%). It is critical therefore to be mindful of how your patterns of behaviour impact on the people around you.
- In his article "Leadership that Gets Results", Daniel Goleman cites how different styles of leadership impact on organizational climate. Adopting and overusing a directive style can have a negative impact on climate, leading to demotivation and disengagement of team members. It does however, have a role to play especially during crisis or immediate time pressures. Using a visionary style, which provides clear direction and enables others to come on that journey has been shown to have a more positive effect. Likewise, a coaching approach has a positive outcome although may not be appropriate in all circumstances.

- We are often required to adapt our management and leadership style but how do you know what to do and in what circumstances?
- This chapter will continue to explore this, but it is essential to recognise that flexibility in your management approach is fundamental to success.

2. Identify behaviours of effective leaders and managers

- The concept of flexibility in styles is important but you may want to take a moment to consider what good management and leadership looks like. Consider leaders and managers you have worked with previously. Ask yourself:
    - o What qualities did you admire?
    - o What was the impact on you and others within the team?
    - o What didn't you like and why?
- Start identifying key behaviours that you believe contribute to good management, truly exploring how that attribute, behaviour or attitude made a difference to you and others within your team. This will help you to create a clearer picture of success and provide you with an opportunity to explore what is important for you in your role.

3. Take time to understand yourself

- Leadership starts with a good understanding of you. Self-awareness is key. You may be clear about the need for flexibility in your style but understanding what is important to you and how you behave on a good day and when under pressure is essential.   This will enable you to respond and adapt your style in different circumstances.
- To be happy and fulfilled, authenticity is vital. Authentic leaders are true to their values rather than responding to the conditions around them.

- You need a strong awareness of your values and how these influence your behaviour.
- This will allow you to evaluate your behaviour and ongoing consider what changes are needed to have a greater impact as a leader.
- The starting point is to ask yourself a series of questions:
  - o What are the core values that drive you and to what extent does your working environment align with them?
  - o Are your values aligned with your behaviours – do you do what you say you will do?
  - o What happens when you are under pressure? Does your style differ and what is the impact of this?
  - o What management styles do you adopt and when? Which do you prefer and why?
- Let's consider an example. Joe's management style is to instruct team members what and how exactly they should complete allocated tasks. He was aware that he is perceived as very directive and staff feel he micro-manages. In a conversation, Joe confirmed that quality is core to his work and getting it right first time was key to being more productive. Compromising on quality is not optional so he manages this by controlling how others work. A coaching conversation with Joe explored how he could work with his team to ensure high quality work was delivered without always using a directive style, thus aligning with his own values and achieving desired outcomes in an alternative, more positive way.

4. Define how you would like to be perceived by others

- Create a vision in your own mind of how you would like to be perceived by others. How would you like to behave every day?
- Being able to articulate what type of leader you want to be and what others would say about you is a fabulous way to bring about any changes you want to make.
- To do this, simply imagine yourself one year from now. It is your annual appraisal. Your manager will want to discuss key progress areas with you. Take a moment to reflect on this and to picture that journey.
  - o What have you achieved this year?
  - o What have your colleagues and team said about you?
  - o What challenges did you overcome to achieve your goals?
- In answering these questions, you will have a clear vision of what you are setting out to do and to become the leader you want to be. Now look at where you are right now. These questions will help you formulate an action plan:
  - o What do I want to do to move forward?
  - o How will I know if I am successful?
  - o What support do I need and from whom?
  - o What steps can I take today, next month and later in the year?
- Finally, to maintain momentum and commitment to your goal, share your plan with someone you trust. If you prefer not to tell someone (ask yourself why) but you could write it down and simply set yourself a forward diary invite to check in with yourself to explore progress.

5. Provide Clarity and Direction

- Having identified your leadership vision, provide clarity and direction to your team. Kouzes and Posner identified five key practices of effective global leaders. One is to "Inspire a Shared Vision". **Shared** meaning you seek to involve your team to contribute and develop the end goal.
- John Kotter, a Harvard Professor, suggests you encourage stakeholders to criticise your ideas because getting people's attention is vital – criticism causes sparks and sparks grab our attention. If people aren't stoked about your idea, it won't succeed
- Building an inspiring vision and making it clear to team members how their work fits into this, supports motivation and is an effective way of driving up every aspect of climate. This approach helps people to understand that what they do matters and why.
- Defining performance standards and clear goals to achieve your desired outcomes is equally important. Challenge can be motivating and leads us to push further. Be mindful that the standards are realistic and achievable. Work with individuals to review progress and feedback to ensure the task is achieved.
- A useful note: Goleman describes the "pacesetter" leadership style, which focuses on high standards for performance and a strong drive to deliver and achieve outcomes. This approach can get quick results from a highly motivated team. A note of caution – avoid "do as I do, now" as this can impact negatively on the team climate. Explore clarity around the task whilst allowing people to consider how they undertake their work.   To do this well, trust is vital. You have to recognise your team's capability and talent.

6. Fostering trust

- Trust between team members is essential to achieve team goals. A lack of trust can lead to behaviours that undermine team performance. Your role is to build this trust and establish an open and honest environment where views can be shared. Successfully harnessing this environment will enable your team to be innovative, creative and productive.
- There are behaviours that build trust with colleagues and team members. Doing what you said you would do is a good starting point. If you commit to something and you were overly ambitious, make sure you are honest about this and renegotiate deadlines or apologise and share your learning about the situation. Displaying vulnerability allows others to recognise that you are not perfect and can still learn.
- It also enables others to come forward and support you, using their strengths and skills to help the team deliver its goals.
- Core skills around listening and asking questions, both used when adopting a coaching style, are vital to build a trusted relationship. When people are listened to, they feel more valued. Listening takes practice. Suspend your own thoughts or judgments and focus on your colleague/employee. Resist "listening to respond" and adopt "listening to understand". The story you hear may not be the issue – you will only find out this through listening. Observe body language and voice tone which improves understanding of that person's issues. Show you are listening by summarising and reflecting back. This also checks you have not misunderstood.
- Consider your own questioning skills. Adopt open questions to discover more about concerns, issues, needs and ideas. Closed questions limit ability for team members to contribute ideas and may result in closing down conversations.

- Being able to explore ideas in a supportive way empowers others and contributes towards trust.

7. Share Power

- We often assume that successful leaders spend their time making decisions, directing commands and using authority to impose their ideas on others. This is however, far from reality. The best leaders gain power by giving it away. Sharing leadership and power motivates team members and keeps them engaged. It creates energy and a climate that generates commitment and engagement in their people. In practice they provide their team with the space to use their own judgment and make decisions.
- Another core leadership practice defined by Kouzes and Posner is "Enable Others to Act". Providing others with the autonomy to do their job, fosters motivation and supports job satisfaction. To do this successfully requires your thoughtful consideration.
- Do not simply pass the task over and forget it. Ensure individuals understand what that task entails, how it fits into the wider objective or vision alongside defined outcomes and expectations and to build accountability. Giving time to team members to clarify expectations and understanding will save you time in the long run.
- Successful leaders know their teams well, allowing effective delegation. Awareness of the different skill sets and capabilities of team members enables selection of the right people when assigning work. Enabling people means they should not feel overwhelmed or under resourced. Adopting a coaching style to understand and support their development has a significant positive impact. A great coach will fundamentally believe the individual has the resources to identify what they need and what is possible.

8. Flexing your style

- Successful leaders flex their approach according to the context they are working in. This may be a specific situation or person. Goleman uses the analogy of trying to play golf with only one type of club. You would be more effective if you used a range of clubs. Likewise, at work the art of flexing and adapting your approach is key to get the best results.
- We have touched on various approaches: coaching, visionary and directive. Adopting an affiliative style focused on building relationships, displaying empathy, strong communication and bringing a team together has a positive impact. Many of the behaviours we have already specified such as listening, asking questions, building trust and rapport will support you to adopt this style. However, an affiliative style can have its disadvantages. Working in a cosy, harmonious team may feel really comfortable and providing you are able to challenge, address difficult issues and maintain high performance standards, then this style is fine. However, if the thought of rocking the boat, challenging the status quo or addressing poor performance concerns you, then you might be stuck in the environment of group think and false harmony
- Be prepared to openly address poor performance. Your role as a leader is to encourage debate and healthy conflict as it leads to better team performance.
- Build time to reflect on your own management style, exploring what techniques and approaches you are using. If you are concerned you have become too affiliative or perhaps, democratic where you are always seeking other views prior to making decisions, then adopt coaching questions to assess where you would like to be:
  - What am I noticing at the moment?
  - What needs to be different?

- o   What would I see / feel / hear if things had changed?
- o   What options could I try to move things forward?
- o   What will I do?

9. Unconscious Bias in your management style

- **Unconscious bias** refers to a bias that we are **unaware of**, happens automatically, is **outside of our control** and triggered by our brain making quick judgements and assessments of people and situations, influenced by our **background, cultural environment** and **personal experiences.** Based on our natural survival mechanism, our brain morphs situations and people into different groups without fully understanding or engaging with them, which leads us to make decisions about those groupings almost instantly. Those quick decisions may not always be right and could lead us to miss out on truly getting the most from team members.
- To mitigate against our unconscious bias, carefully consider the decisions you make taking a brief moment to question your first impressions about someone. You may find you are dismissing an idea or viewpoint, perhaps not truly listening to the other person because you believe your idea is right. In fact, this may well be confirmation bias emerging. And to be fair, you might be right in your view.
- As a manager, are you openly listening to others and providing a space for different views to be shared or are you dismissing it before properly considering the options?
- Ultimately, humans are biased. We have a tendency to favour individuals who we have an affinity with or we see as similar to ourselves. However, your role is to build inclusivity, maximising skill mix and learning across the team.

It is critical to consider how bias may be impacting on your decisions and judgments.

10. Take a step back

- Discipline yourself to make time to reflect and take a step back to consider your approaches. Everyone should do this as it is so easy to become embroiled in the day-to-day activity and inadvertently continue with the same habits that do not always facilitate the most effective outcomes. You do not need huge amounts of time to do this, rather a couple of minutes post meetings or at the end of the day. Some questions to consider:
    - o What approaches have I used as manager?
    - o What was the impact? Is there anything I might do differently next time?
- Seek feedback. As a manager you are building your own awareness and understanding of how you behave, particularly under stress. You can use formal opportunities - your appraisal or performance review - to gather feedback from team members and peers. Look for opportunities to invite feedback throughout the year. The more you encourage feedback this will facilitate a culture where feedback becomes the norm.
- Get your own coach. Your management journey is unlikely to be an easy one, but it can be very fulfilling. Leading people can however be challenging and working with an impartial coach can help you to challenge your thinking, behaviours and approach in different circumstances.
- Coaching and reflecting may provide you with an opportunity to gain insight into your own preferences as a leader and how your style may be helpful or unhelpful at times.
- Trust between team members is essential to achieve team goals.

A lack of trust can lead to behaviours that undermine team performance. Your role is to build this trust and establish an open and honest environment where views can be shared.

- Successfully harnessing this environment will enable your team to be innovative, creative and productive.
- There are behaviours that build trust with colleagues and team members. Doing what you said you would do is a good starting point. If you commit to something and you were overly ambitious, make sure you are honest about this and renegotiate deadlines or apologise and share your learning about the situation. Displaying vulnerability allows others to recognise that you are not perfect and can still learn.
- It also enables others to come forward and support you, using their strengths and skills to help the team deliver its goals.
- Core skills around listening and asking questions, both used when adopting a coaching style, are vital to build a trusted relationship. When people are listened to, they feel more valued. Listening takes practice. Suspend your own thoughts or judgments and focus on your colleague/employee. Resist "listening to respond" and adopt "listening to understand". The story you hear may not be the issue – you will only find out this through listening. Observe body language and voice tone which improves understanding of that person's issues. Show you are listening by summarising and reflecting back. This also checks you have not misunderstood.
- Consider your own questioning skills. Adopt open questions to discover more about concerns, issues, needs and ideas.
Closed questions limit ability for team members to contribute ideas and may result in closing down conversations.
- Being able to explore ideas in a supportive way empowers others and contributes towards trust.

YOUR NOTES FROM CHAPTER 5

Chapter 6

Top 10 Tips about how to incorporate coaching techniques into your management role

By Ian Munro

It is a common trend that following a coaching programme the person being coached feels positive about their outcomes and would like to introduce to their workplace a number of the coaching techniques from which they personally benefited. How do they transfer these benefits to other colleagues?

Let's define management. To me people manage in three different areas; people, processes and projects. These could be one of the above in isolation or a blend of two or three.

Firstly people; I have coached people running large teams of over 100 people (through a number of line managers). Secondly; people who are subject matter experts who have few or no direct reports but need to have an impact on senior people several grades higher than them. Thirdly; project managers who have no direct reports but have a dotted line team reporting to them who can have a number of different projects running of which theirs is one of them.

Understanding the different coaching styles will help you apply coaching methodologies in your workplace.

1.   Aligning yourself to the meaning, behaviours and types of coaching

- Broadly speaking we are looking at different styles of coaching – executive and management coaching which can include Directive and Non-Directive coaching. These two are further defined in points 2 and 3 below.
- Other types of coaching include
   - Career Coaching – the longer-term career planning and development of the talent pool
   - Performance Coaching – aimed at correctly or developing particular areas of personal development aligned to the needs of the employing organisation

- o Skills Coaching – Even tighter in focus than Performance Coaching, Skills Coaching aims to correct skills shortfalls in the coachee as a result of a Career Path Needs Skills Inventory
- o Business Coaching – the focus here is on learnings about the commercial aspects and needs of the organisation and a programme of coaching to address shortfalls on the part of the coachee. Examples of this could be a deeper understanding of how Finance impacts on the organisation, or aspects of Marketing
- o Life coaching – not normally popular for sponsorship in organisations as this addresses the individual's life style needs, not the organisation

2. Directive Coaching

This form of coaching applies where there is a specific need to blend coaching with guidance and advice. Typical examples are;

- Training – The coaching piece is part of the training topic where the coachee would for example be asked to create their action plan past the training, or to address how the coachee will deal with anticipated on the job issues and challenges.
- Advising – This is getting close to being overly directive and any element of coaching disappears. By all means discuss options with the coachee but try to leave the option decision to them.
- Giving feedback – This a great way to introduce coaching.
- Based on what the coachee has produced your feedback can be blended with questions about what they have done, what improvement could they make, timescales going forward etc. etc.

- Offering suggestions – be wary that suggestions imply your solution to the topic and not theirs. It key with this form of coaching that the decision on action be theirs.

3. Non-Directive coaching

- This type of coaching is all about asking questions and listening, creating the environment where the coachee has a chance to reflect, think and be guided by the coach's technique. Often this type would be seen as the standard approach for executive and management coaching.
- Here are some broad issues to consider when considering using this in your management role.
- Remember we are not having a formal coaching session, just using some of the tools and approaches.
  o Purpose – is it for your benefit or your colleagues?
  o Be clear about what you want out of the discussion
  o Take the other party's needs into account
  o Setting – where are you going to have the chat
  o Might be informal to be in a café area -what about the disruptive noise from the coffee machine?
  o Is the setting suitable for creative discussion?
  o Will the other party be comfortable and relaxed, so you can get the best outcomes?
- Meeting expectations – yours and theirs
  o Has this been established before you meet?
  o Do you believe you will get a better result "playing it off the cuff?

- Documenting decisions –
  - o Coachees normally take the notes, but you will have to on this occasion
  - o Don't take meeting minutes, just note the decisions or future actions, by whom and when
- The follow up – making sure what has been agreed is fulfilled
  - o The "coaching style" discussion should have led to your colleague taking action. Did you agree a follow up session?
  - o Are there actions for you by certain date/time?

4. Creating a platform and style for your coaching approach with team and colleagues

- The secret here is that your colleagues should not feel that you are coaching them. So, your style needs to reflect this.
- By colleagues I mean those at the three levels in workplace relationships – your peers, those more senior than you and those more junior than you. Each level requires a slightly different approach – see outlines below.
- Sometimes in our coaching work we are helping coachees to resolve where a coaching approach with colleagues has gone wrong. Some of the answers are below.
- **Your peers** – although whilst at the same level as you in the organisation one of the challenges about peer relationships is that they can be multi-functional across many disciplines – finance, marketing, operations etc. Different types of roles have the habit of recruiting people with behaviours and style common to that role.

For example, the sales team will be different to the operations team. This means that you will need a style and approach that flexes according to the peers you are with. One style will not fit all.

- **Those more senior** – Without being over deferential, you want your more senior contacts to agree and support you in terms of achieving an objective by getting their support. Ask for their support pointing out how the project activity will benefit them. Too often managers forget that their managers need support too.
- **Those more junior** – these people are your engine room, the ones whose action will help you achieve your goals. Seek their opinions and ideas, give them air time, support and encourage them by listening and questioning. Feed them slivers of your ideas hoping they will latch onto them and adopt them for their use and your benefit.

5.   **Setting your own coaching goals and timing from this process**

- Having been coached you will be all too aware of the goal setting and performance measuring part of the coaching process. These were fundamental to the success of your programme.
- Now with the aim of introducing elements of your coaching into your day to day work what goals and sub goals are you going to set yourself.
- **The Learning Zone** contains a goal and sub goals planning tool – Action Plan - which will be helpful.
- Because you are using these coaching techniques in your day to day work try to set time scales that are achievable and not too ambitious. You are adopting a new approach which will also rely on inputs from others.

If the timescales are too tough you will get slippage and disappointment. Better to set more realistic achievable times which will bring to others a sense of achievement.

6. **Setting goals and timing for individuals and teams**

- One of the features that will have made your coaching programme a success was the way in which your coach steered you to create and develop the steps to achieving your goals, acting as a listening post and sounding board.
- We suggest that you adopt a similar approach with individuals and teams. Especially with teams it is a powerful tool to allow them – with certain guidelines - to create the goals and timing that meet your own goals and timing.
- Having created the goals, they will have the ownership and peer pressure to meet goal and timing targets.
- As stated in point 5 above make sure that they are setting reasonable and achievable goals otherwise you will have a demotivated team to handle.
- **The Learning Zone** contains a goal and sub goals action planning tool which will be helpful.

7. **Individual and group challenges**

Some things are being repeated here but I need to remind you this is not about individual and group coaching but how having brought coaching into these situations do you deal with the challenges. These challenges below apply to individuals and groups.

- Goal slippage – Because there is not the sharpness to the goals and their achievement of a formal coaching environment there can be a tendency for slippage. Agree regular reviews/updates which will keep things on track.
- Keeping focus – the wider organisation is (hopefully) steaming ahead and it is easy to get distracted. Team gatherings, blogs, etc. are ways to keep the other distractions at bay.
- Weakest link – There will always be someone in a group, who is slower than the others, meaning that they may need extra support to keep up with others. The Action Plan mentioned above will help in dealing with this challenge.
- Outside influencers – Other colleagues and often those more senior will have their agendas too. Try to get their buy-in to support your initiatives. Be aware and keep close if there are sending your team off course.

8.   Checking and reviewing progress

- How is adapting coaching into your management role working for you – you have set yourself and others goals and time targets? How often are they being reviewed?
- Have you asked for feedback from your line manager – what do they think of your approach in introducing coaching techniques?
- Do they consider it is working? What impact are you making at large?
- Can they support you with senior managers at their level?
- If you have a Mentor, ask for their feedback.

- If the approach is working and you have managers with their own teams, are they able to cascade your approach with them?

9.   Communicating outputs in your organisation

- How do you communicate your success without being accused of self-aggrandisement?
- If your team is doing well get them to blow the trumpet!
- Generally, you have promoted a collegiate style that has improved your team's performance and benefited the organisation. Get the team to write regular Blogs via Internal Comms department.
- Of course, if you do not want to shout from the rooftops that is fine too.
- Make sure your team recognises the changes for the better they have made.

10.   Some tools to help you along the way

- With all the other documents we need to maintain in our working lives, we do not want to overload you with many more.
- However, there are some which are relevant to coaching and which will help you to manage coaching in the workplace. These are explained below, and examples of these tools can be seen in the Learning Zone.
- Basic Coaching agreement – You should have seen a document like this if you have been on a coaching programme. The purpose of this document is that if you want to incorporate coaching techniques into your work place, you need to have some form of written agreement between you and your colleagues.

This can range from the example document shown or just listing the goals development areas and results. There is strong evidence from the coaching world that coaching effectiveness is really improved when the goals etc. are documented.

- Quarterly Coaching Action Plan – The aim here is that the colleague you are working with has a way of listing their Goals and Development Areas and has to list their planned actions via a number of tasks at the beginning of the quarter. As the quarter unfolds they have an Outcome box which means they can list progress. This is a very simple document which works well for many people. Some use this document on a monthly basis because they are working to shorter timescales. All you need to do is change the title from Quarterly to Monthly.

YOUR NOTES FROM CHAPTER 6

Chapter 7

Top 10 Tips for coaching teams and groups

By Mark Greenfield

In this chapter, we argue that collective and collaborative leadership is critical to enable teams to be functioning, effective and self-motivating. Focused team coaching has emerged in recent years as a fundamental series of approaches to enable leaders to transform and optimise performance.

Described here are a series of reflections, interventions, techniques and practical strategies that will enable you to coach groups of people, whether a defined 'team', group, virtual or project team and if you are their manager or brought in to work with the team.

1. What is a Team?

- A team is any group of people organised to work together interdependently and cooperatively to accomplish a purpose or a goal: "... *a small number of people with complementary skills who are committed to a common purpose, performance goals, and approach for which they hold themselves mutually accountable*" (from 'The Wisdom of Teams' by Katzenbach & Smith). So, ask if a 'team' is necessary for the achievement of goals and tasks? What is the added value that a 'team' could bring?

- What is the optimum size team for maximising Performance? This is influenced by several factors: the purpose for which you formed the team; the expectations you have of the team and its members; the roles that the team members need to play and the responsibilities each are given. Research by Michael West at Aston Business School and by others has highlighted that in general, the optimum team size is 5 - 7 members.

- The team size that continues to function effectively is 4 - 9 members. Numbers higher than 12 will often result in informal sub-teams forming and this may hinder effective communication.
- What is the value of a high performing team? There is abundant evidence in the literature that enabling teams to form and flourish is a 'good thing' for both business and people and has been demonstrated across all sectors. Some of the benefits offered by successful teams are:
  - More planning, relating individual activities to the total objective
  - Less defensiveness in meetings
  - Greater involvement in projects
  - Paying more attention to looking at forward objectives
  - Increased innovation
  - Reduced staff turnover
  - Allowing greater reliance on each other, sharing a common view of objectives
  - Adaptability to changing circumstances and pressures
  - Achieving more in productivity
- Is your team clear on what effective teamwork can achieve? What are their opinions on how it functions currently?

2.   Context for Team Coaching – Understanding Group Behaviour

Group behaviour is never predictable, even if you know all the individuals well. Look for the following signs, learn to recognise situations and you will be able to deal with any issues whilst they are relatively small and resolvable:

- The difference between content and process:
  When individuals in groups communicate, there are two major ingredients operating: Content - the subject matter on which they are operating, and Process - what's happening between the individuals. If, as a team or group leader you only focus on the Content, you will miss picking up on the Process, including the atmosphere created, potential areas of conflict and emotions between individuals, which is often a major source of conflict in groups. What do you need to do to focus more on process?
- How decisions are made:
  - Look out for what happens when information is exchanged, and the group is trying to arrive at a decision.
  - Are decisions made from a logical/rational point of view, or an emotional one?
  - Do decisions arrive from a consensus involving everyone or because one or two individuals dominate the conversation?
  - How as a team coach can you focus more closely on how decisions are made?
  - What do you need to look for?
- How people are influenced:
  Remember that influence and participation are not the same. Some individuals may be frequent contributors but are rarely acknowledged, whereas others may talk much less but are listened to when they do. Influence can take many forms, so try to observe which styles others use:

- o *Autocrats* attempt to impose his/her will on others and often only think of themselves
- o *Peacemakers* aim to prevent conflict or expression of unpleasant feelings at all costs by pouring oil on troubled waters
- o *Laidback* people seem withdrawn and uninvolved, responding only if asked and may be dominated by others
- o *Democrats* work hard to include everyone in the discussion or decision

How does influence work in your team? What do you need to change?

- As a team coach, working with front-line teams, through to senior management teams, and Boards, I regularly work with several models and frameworks to support teams to achieve their goals. There are three approaches that I find particularly useful.

3.   Team Coaching Diagnostic I

- Peter Hawkins, in his book Leadership Team Coaching (Kogan Page, 2011) describes his effective team coaching model as 'the five disciplines of successful team practice':

  1. Commissioning: clarifying goals and success measures is critical for whoever is responsible for commissioning the team.
  2. Clarifying: once the team has been commissioned, understanding and agreeing their mission is important to achieve ownership.
  3. Co-creating: the team deciding how they will constructively work together is vital to ensure the focus is on what works rather than what doesn't.

4   Connecting: how the team relates to all partners and key stakeholders determines how well they focus on their performance.

5   Core learning: this is central to all four disciplines and is characterised by the team regularly reviewing how well they are functioning and are fit for purpose.

- How well does your team function as a 'team'? Have you built in regular time to review team functionality?

4.   Team Coaching Diagnostic II

Patrick Lencioni described 'The Five Dysfunctions of a Team' clearly in his Leadership Fable (Jossey Bass, 2002).

- The framework is a well-documented evidence-based approach to team development which uses practical interventions and tools which can be applied to each level in a relatively short time scale and monitored for effectiveness.

Effective teams will demonstrate the following outcomes:

- Have **high levels of trust** such that each team member is willing to expose their individual weaknesses and vulnerabilities to other team members without fear of exploitation.
  That trust gives team members security to have **robust and unfiltered conflict** around key ideas.
- As a result, there is full and **collective commitment to plans of action**, even if there isn't full agreement, because everyone's voice has been heard.
- There is a culture rather than a system of **accountability with peers** holding each other to account.
- They **focus on collective results** rather than individual results or status.
- How well does your team rate in each of these five core behaviours currently? What are your priorities as a team coach?

5.   Team Coaching Diagnostic III

- Semi-structured team diagnostic interviews are often used to ascertain the views of individual team members about their team in a confidential discussion, either face to face or on the telephone, prior to a team timeout. Views on successful outcomes for the team, feedback on how well the team functions, and suggestions for improving the way the team works in the future can be established in a space that often allows individuals to 'open up' and be more honest. A synopsis of the conversations and an analysis of the key themes that have emerged during the process will be fed back to the team at the timeout. Key lines of enquiry might include:

- o Considering your team, what are you pleased about or proud of about how you work together currently?
- o What can you do to build on your strengths?
- o What is less good or challenging about how you work together?
- o What are your team weaknesses?
- o What do you need to stop or do less of?
- o What are the priorities for you in terms of team development at the timeout?
- How ready is your team for a development Timeout? Would semi-structured interviews in advance be helpful?

6. Coaching to improve Trust and Relationships in Teams

- Good team coaches connect with everyone in the team. That means moving beyond the superficial to understand individual strengths and weaknesses. For your team to respond well to you as a coach, they must trust you. After all, you're asking them to be introspective, and open or 'vulnerable' enough to discuss how they can maximise their potential.
- A good way to gain trust is to demonstrate that you are actively listening. This means really concentrating on what is being said, and actively stating that you understand their perspective, by playing back what you have heard. Empathy, eye contact and making the environment comfortable for the team member is crucial. Hold one-on-one meetings and, during your discussion, take note. Then give an accurate summary of what your team member told you (rather than just repeating your end of the discussion). This shows that you're genuinely interested in what they have to say and invested in their personal development.

- With team timeouts, use the opportunity to help team members to become more open with each other by encouraging personal stories such as: What are your favourite things to do outside work?
- Share something not many people know about you? Where did you grow up? What was your first job? How can people get the best out of me? Disclosure, whilst slightly uncomfortable at first is a cornerstone to build trust.

7. Coaching for Motivation and Team Resilience

- In 'The Five Practices of Exemplary Leadership' (Kouzes and Posner; The Leadership Challenge; 3rd Ed 2002; Jossey-Bass), Jim Kouzes and Barry Posner describe Enabling Others to Act, and Encouraging the Heart as critical to empowering individuals to find their own motivations.
- Enabling Others to Act means using the word 'We' rather than 'I' and adopting a collaborative approach, focusing on the means not the ends. Collaboration is the master skill that enable teams, alliances and partnerships to 'self-manage' and function effectively. It means developing cooperative relationships with those you work with, actively listening to diverse points of view, promoting cooperative goals and above all, taking time to build trust.
- Encouraging the Heart is in my experience, the most difficult team coaching behaviour to sustain, as it is often sacrificed when the pressure is on the team, and the organisation is challenged. It means recognising individual and team contributions by showing appreciation for extra effort and performance and praising people for a job well done.

It is about letting people know you have confidence in their abilities and encouraging them to experiment and step outside of their comfort zone without fear of blame if things go wrong and using the opportunity to learn instead.

8.   Coaching to encourage Accountability

• Accountability in teams means the willingness of team members to remind one another when they are not living up to the agreed performance standards and behaviours of the group. This shouldn't always require the participation of the team leader, and in high-performing teams the team coach's role is often to encourage direct, peer-to-peer accountability. This is based on the principle that peer pressure and the desire not to let a colleague down will motivate a team member more than any concern over sanctions or rebuke.

• How do we encourage teams where people hold one another accountable? The key is coaching team members to be comfortable in giving each other appreciative *and critical* feedback. This can often be encouraged by helping people to realise that when they fail to provide peers with constructive feedback, they are letting them down personally.

• One way of encouraging a culture of peer-to-peer accountability is to carry out a simple Team Effectiveness Exercise as described by Lencioni in 'Overcoming the Five Dysfunctions of a Team: A Field Guide (2005, Jossey-Bass). This should only be used with teams that have worked together for at least a few months and where there is a degree of trust. During a timeout or away day, ask everyone on the team to write down the answers to two simple questions about every member of the team, excluding themselves:

'What is the single most important behavioural characteristic or quality demonstrated by this person that contributes to the strength of the team?', and 'What is the single most important behavioural characteristic or quality demonstrated by this person that can sometimes derail the team?'

The team coach then starts with the leader and asks each team member to read out their positive qualities about the leader, then their constructive feedback about their potential 'derailing' qualities. This provides direct, honest and unequivocal feedback, and the same process is then repeated for each team member. The outcome is a sharing of positive qualities and development opportunities in a short period of time and can be motivating, constructive and cathartic ... and often all at the same time!

9.   Coaching for Team Performance

As a Team Coach, your top priority may be to facilitate the team to improve their performance. Key interventions that work in addition to the enabling and encouraging behaviours described earlier include:

- Provide frequent, regular feedback and recognition. Annual performance reviews don't give team members all the encouragement they need. At least once a week, team coaches should give their team members informal feedback about areas they need to work on, and recognition for things they're doing well.
- Align employee behaviours to long-term business objectives of the organisation. All teams are trying to achieve something greater than themselves and reach big, long-term goals by working together.

Great managers understand that and use this overarching goal to motivate people and get the best performance by ensuring every team member can see how their performance contributes to the overall growth of the organisation.

- Give team members autonomy and room for personal growth. Managers often struggle with this, but autonomy is one of the most valuable things you can give employees. Don't micromanage your team by telling them how to do things; allow them the freedom to make mistakes that can help them learn and grow.

10. Coaching Teams: An outline for a one-day development workshop

Session 1: Why is there a Need for a team workshop?
- What themes do you need to discuss? For example:
  - o Needing a vision or direction?
  - o Undergoing major change?
  - o Newly-formed and needing to clarify roles and responsibilities?
  - o Agreeing an operational plan?

Session 2: What are the team's Goals?
- Where would the team like to be in 6 months / 1 year / 3 years?
- What will the team be achieving then that they are not achieving now?
- What will achieving these goals do for individuals?
- How will that make them feel?

Session 3: Where is the team Now?
- What achievements are the team most proud of?
- What are the strengths the team can build on now?
- What have been the biggest challenges, and what has the team not done so well?
- What should the team stop doing?

Session 4: What are the Options for Action that the team needs to consider from sessions 2 and 3?

- How will the team decide on the options to take forward?
- What are the key priorities going forward to progress towards team goals?
- What are the specific Actions required and first steps?
- Who needs to lead on what actions and by when?
- How will the team support each other?

YOUR NOTES FROM CHAPTER 7

Part 3

How to choose the best coaches for your organisation

Chapter 8

Top 10 Tips for the Key Areas for Consideration

By Mike Nelson

Some of the points in this chapter have been addressed in earlier chapters. However this is the first of three chapters aimed at helping in the selection of a coach or coaching organisation who will work with your colleagues. Making the right choice is a critical decision. Hopefully we will have been of assistance in choosing the right coaching organisation.

Choosing a coach or coaching organisation can feel like looking for a needle in a haystack, even though there are thousands of needles in the stack.

This chapter aims to break down the variety of questions one might need to ask if you are looking for a coach for yourself or for one or more individuals in your organisation.

You may not need to consider everything mentioned in this chapter, depending on the individual circumstances in which you are selecting a coach but at the very least you can see on a quick read whether you should be asking any questions relating to these topics.

1.   The Chemistry Conversation

•   This is an opportunity for the coachee and one (or more) potential coaches to speak with each other. The aim is to establish the early relationship and for both parties to get some 'measure' of each other. They may meet face to face, by phone or perhaps via electronic media (such as Skype). Such a session should at least contain personal introductions and sharing of backgrounds, an exchange of views of how the coach works (including style/approach) and the expectations and past experiences of coaching from the coachee. There would also normally be a discussion on the initial aims of the work and an opportunity for the coachee to ask any questions they have on their mind.

- Both will leave the session with an initial impression of how they would get on, the style of the coach and with both parties having enough information to indicate whether this particular coaching relationship will work.

- Depending on how many coaches the coachee has seen/spoken with, the follow up is for the coachee to decide which coach would be their preference. In this respect they may need the support of internal advice, usually the individual who has initiated the process in the first place. The coachee should be encouraged to choose the coach with whom they believe they can work (not necessarily the 'easiest' relationship) and who will provide them with the both challenge and support to move towards the desired outcomes for the work.

- It may seem to the reader that this whole process is both subjective as well as objective and this is indeed what it should be. Effective coaching outcomes can be as dependent on the relationship between the coach and coachee just as much as they may depend on the skill and method of the coach.

2.   Coach Matching

- This is a process that will vary in size and scale depending on the size and scale of the organisation and budget etc., indeed in small scale projects may not take place at all. At the very least the organisation may issue a specification for the coaching requirement including experience and/or accreditation required.

- At its widest, the process could involve either individual coaches or coaching organisations being invited to a Coach Matching Process.
- Typically, this would include some background on the organisation, the organisational need for coaching, the specification and requirements for the coaches; giving enough information for the coaches and/or their organisations to be able to decide the appropriateness of providing coaching at the size/scale required and to be able to meet the organisational needs. Often, there would be assessment of the potential coaching 'pool' which could include structured interviewing or even observed demonstrations of coaches at work allowing the organisation to make a more informed choice of the coaches and coaching skills on offer.
- On a smaller scale, coaches may be presented to potential coachees via a selection of coaching profiles or vlogs allowing the coachee to choose an individual or shortlist of those coaches with whom they may want a Chemistry Conversation.

3.   The Role of Supervision

- I mentioned the possible requirement for accreditation of coaches (section 2) but in the longer term it should be considered that whilst accreditation may give an indication of entry competence, it is only the process of effective supervision whereby a coach would maintain/improve their practice and professional standards over time.

- Supervision allows the coach to be able to explore and develop their learning and competence through reflective practise, to further develop their practise and ensure they stay up to date with the advancement of the profession.
- Also having a safe/confidential place to discuss the challenges/stresses of coaching with others.
- The frequency of supervision will depend on the needs of the individual coach and on the amount/intensity of the coaching they are undertaking. Typically, a coach would go to Supervision three/four times a year.

4.   Evaluation

- Coaching is often one of the more expensive development interventions you can provide as in many cases it is one-on-one and will require a number of interventions depending on the needs and requirements of the coachee(s). This will mean that the sponsoring/budget-holding department would want to get an understanding of the return on investment for such interventions.
- The coaching programme may of course be part of a much wider structured development programme (such as a blended learning leadership programme) and therefore the evaluation of the coaching would form part of the overall evaluation of the total programme. Measures of individual change and progress, application of learning, demonstration of organisational change and/or business results could all be included and there are a variety of well-used methods for collecting such data such as evaluation questionnaires or forms, focus groups, structured interviews etc.

- Any of these broader methods in the larger programmes should try and gain some differential impact of the delivery methods being used to gain insight into the effectiveness of the various components.
- Build in evaluation at the start, even if it is a single coachee and a short intervention at least some demonstration of the learning by the coachee, changes of behaviour, application to the organisation/department and the impact of the intervention would be useful measures to demonstrate the effectiveness of an intervention.

5. Feedback

- One of the biggest challenges for coaches is knowing whether the coachee is presenting the whole of the issue they are working on; very often a coach might be relying on the coachees own point of view. It would therefore be useful if feedback from other parties could be obtained to use in the coaching programme.
- Feedback can be collected in a variety of ways, by the coach, the coachee or using a process such as 360/180° feedback. The effectiveness of using an external coach can be greatly enhanced if feedback is incorporated into the process.
- Some coaches, (I'm amongst those) will also offer to observe the coachee at work. This can provide a rich source of additional feedback and observation for the coach to work with. It also helps the coach see the coachee in context and this can be quite different from sitting in a somewhat sterile meeting room.

It will not always be possible due to the nature of the coachees work but if it is possible then it should be considered as part of the overall plan.

6. Learning from your Coaches

- From an organisational perspective, having coaches work within the organisation could provide a very valuable source of organisational learning. It is often ignored and could provide an insightful source of data about how the organisation works at a behavioural level.

- There is an important factor to note here – getting coaches to report on behavioural trends, organisational culture etc., must not compromise the confidentiality of individual coachees. Any data collected must be anonymous, should be a reasonable sample size (so to prevent identifying one of a small number of individuals) and specific examples which may break confidentiality will not be included.

- For a larger coaching intervention, with a number of coaches it may prove very useful to gather them together at intervals and ask for things they have noticed about organisational behaviours and culture which may pave the way for future training interventions or Organisational Development work within the organisation itself.

7. Pricing

- Well how long is a piece of string? I've already mentioned in this chapter that coaching can be one of the most expensive interventions that can be made...

Because it is one-on-one, takes time and it is hard to measure in a fully objective way how do you know how much to pay for a coach.

- The one thing I won't do is quote specifics, the marketplace is so variable, organisations budgets so vastly different and any price quoted would soon make this book obsolete.

- What can be said is that a budget should be set. Expect to pay more for more experienced coaches, and in general pay more for executive/board level coaches. Get quotes from different coaches; it may be very useful to contrast charges by coaching organisations compared to self-employed coaches. Talk to purchasers in organisations similar to yours – what do they pay or expect to pay? It is worth remembering that reputable coaches will have invested in their development and accreditation, pay for Supervision and Professional Development as well as overheads such as professional indemnity insurance etc. Coaches provided by coaching organisations will also invoke on-cost as the provider needs to make a margin too. Check if travel is included or is a rechargeable extra.

- If all the quotes you get are outside budget, then there are possible ways of reducing cost. Using telephone-based coaching (or technology based such as Skype) and limiting the time allowed for coaching (some coaching organisations offer short telephone-based interventions of, say, 30 minutes per coachee to keep budget down). Do remember however that a principle of "you get what you pay for" also operates here.

- Good quality, reputable coaches who are experienced and effective will often be a very effective way of providing such focused and bespoke development rather than sending staff on numerous training courses often with little impact or retention of learning.

8.   How long should it be?

- To some extent this section overlaps with the budget management ideas discussed in section 7 above. Typically, a series of 1:1 coaching interventions will take the form of 3 or 6 sessions taking place at intervals of 4-6 weeks with individual sessions lasting between 1-2 hours. Having said this there will be a wide range of variations around the programme quoted and this can depend on the availability of the manager to be released, how the organisation wishes to deploy coaches and whether coaches will visit or work by phone or Skype.
- One methodology is for a coach to provide a "Coaching Clinic" – in this case they may be deployed and available for a day (or half day) where managers can book 'slots' of 30-45 minutes – this can be a cost-effective way of utilising a coaching resource inside your organisation. It would not be appropriate however for coachees with more complex or deep needs.
- It is worth asking potential coaches how long they recommend coaches sessions should last – this will give you an idea of their MO as a coach and will help you evaluate whether they are most suited to the kind of intervention your organisation needs.

9. Setting Objectives

- This may seem an obvious part of the process and in many cases the coachee working towards a set of defined objectives would be a normal part of any coaching contract/intervention.
  Often objectives for coaching will be tied in with Personal Development Plans (PDPs). If objectives are to be set, to tie in with the whole philosophy of effective coaching, then the coachee should think for themselves what the objectives should be even if they are subsequently reviewed by line manager and/or HR.

- Having said this there is a school of thought that coaching objectives can actually get in the way of effective, free-flowing coaching where emergence is a rich source of finding the real problem and/or the creative solution.

- When objectives are set, do allow at least for review and an evolving picture so that new thinking, information can be taken into account when trying to obtain real/effective change for your organisation.

10. Three-Way Conversations (with line managers)

- Coaches will often talk of the coaching contract, this is both a written and unwritten agreement between the coach and coachee which defines the scope, scale and boundaries for the work. It may also include the practicalities of time, location and evaluation as mentioned elsewhere in this chapter as well as any ground rules and important factors such as coachee confidentiality.

- In organisations where the origination and/or sponsorship comes from a line manager it is good practise to involve the line manager and coachee in a 3-way conversation with the coachee.
- This allows for the line manager and the coachee to agree objective or aims for the coaching, for any feedback from the line manager to be discussed in front of the coach and allows the coach to ask any relevant questions to this conversation to enter the coaching process with as clear a brief as possible.
- It may also be useful to have a three-way conversation with the line manager at the halfway stage and at the end. This would allow for some practical evaluation of progress and any further feedback from the line manager to be delivered in earshot of the coach.

YOUR NOTES FROM CHAPTER 8

Chapter 9

Top 10 Tips for Understanding the importance of Coaching Supervision

By Dawn Scott

Coaching is still as yet an unregulated profession, unlike other similar roles in counselling, psychotherapy and often physical therapies, where you are required to demonstrate evidence of continuing professional development (CPD) and undertake what is known as 'supervision' in order to practice.

Supervision for the caring professions offers the practitioner an opportunity to reflect on their experiences with clients, the psychological processes observed and the impact of their interventions on themselves and their clients. Coaching organisations such as The International Coaching Federation (ICF) or European Mentoring and Coaching Council (EMCC) require their accredited coaches to follow their own guidelines on supervision and demonstrate regular attendance as part of their reflective practice.

The best coaching providers follow the ethical guidelines set out by these organisations and this chapter explains why supervision is important to assure the quality of coaching that you are seeking for your employees.

1. **Understanding Coaching Supervision – some definitions**

- The British Association of Counselling & Psychotherapy (BACP) in their first document on supervision (1987) stated that: *"The primary purpose of supervision is to protect the best interests of the client"*.
- More specifically Loganbill et al (1982) said that supervision was *"An intensive interpersonally focused, one-to-one relationship in which one person is designated to facilitate the development of therapeutic competence in the other person"*.
- Proctor (1988a) described the main processes in the supervision of counselling in terms of *formative, restorative* and *normative.*

- *Formative* is the function of education such that the supervisor enables the coach in this case, through reflection and exploration of the issues presented.
- The *Restorative* or supportive function is where the coach may have been engaged in very intensive sessions with clients and have been affected by the client's distress. In this case they need to understand how and why that has come about and how they can manage that in future sessions.
- Finally, the *Normative* function is how the coach upholds the standards of their coaching for clients. This is where the supervisor ensures that the coach understands where these standards are breached or where the ethics of their approach may be challenged. The supervisor in this case carries some responsibility for the client Hawkins (2000).

2. How will my organisation benefit from coaching supervision?

- Coaching Providers who deliver coaching supervision are acting as responsible suppliers of their services firstly for the direct benefit of individual clients and secondly to sponsor organisations that are funding coaching contract for their people.
- It is a mark of quality assurance for any purchaser of coaching services. It says that the coach values themselves and their practice to assure you the client that they will take care of your people.
- Coaching aims to improve the productivity of your people and providers whose coaches undertake supervision will be up to date with current thinking, be confident and reflective practitioners and therefore more likely to deliver a return on investment for your people.

- Whilst coaching is different say to psychotherapy, there are often occasions when clients disclose sometimes traumatic life experiences which have influenced behaviour traits that are being displayed in the workplace that may be inhibiting progress for that individual. Coaches are not immune to this and supervision should give you the assurance that they know how to handle themselves in those situations and how to deal with their clients. Supervision enables safe and ethical practice therefore.

3.   What types of supervision should I consider?

- If you are a coach it is important to have access to 1:1 supervision at regular intervals during your coaching contracts. Usually this is one supervision hour to every 6-8 coaching sessions.
- Accredited coaches will have to ensure that the expected standards of supervision meet with their association's guidelines.
- Group supervision is a minimum requirement for any ethical coach provider where coaches have a regular group session with a few colleagues and a qualified coach supervisor.
- Learning from other colleagues is a helpful addition to this approach a little like action learning where you can be questioned by others on your approach to a situation.

Peer Supervision is often an approach that fits in with the helping professions work patterns and is a useful bonding activity within teams.

It may not offer all of the three supervision functions as mentioned earlier (_formative, restorative & normative_) but is still part of reflective practice which allows challenge and support to the practitioner.

4. How to set up supervision to promote a coaching culture

- External coaching providers should be able to demonstrate to you how their coaching providers obtain supervision through either formal accreditation or company standards or policies. You may want to seek further assurance through the confirmation of CPD certificates obtained or supervision records.
- If you have a pool of coaches within your organisation that you have invested in training for, it is an essential requirement that you provide opportunities at least group supervision for them. You can choose to invest further in external providers of coaching supervision or in training one or two of your current coaches in the role of coach supervisor.
- It is important to recognise the pros and cons of using internal coaches and often it is helpful to have some independent input to provide an outlet for issues of concern so external supervision may be a helpful way of providing that for your internal coaches and to help staff see the link that supports the confidentiality of the coaching contract for them as clients.
- Finally, where you may have developed a coaching approach for line managers or as a behaviour set for all staff, it may not be absolutely necessary for formal supervision but a helpful addition to the business to provide additional support through say action learning groups to promote peer support.

5. Developing a Learning Culture

- Coaching Supervision in this context is a good indicator that you are developing a learning culture for your business.

- Reflective practitioners or developing processes that encourage reflection on learning signifies to your customers that quality assurance is key to everything you do.
- Whilst the price of goods and services is often cited as the key to retaining your market share, however quality differentiates the good from the great whether in product or service terms. If you work in highly regulated industries, then quality is paramount in allowing you to continue to operate in that market place. Supervision in line with your business culture will assure your customers of that quality.
- It is valuable therefore to offer a range of CPD activities that reflect on the level of informal and formal coaching that happens in your organisation; supervision is just one offer.

6.   Supervision Processes

- Hawkins seven-eyed model of supervision is a well-known systematic and comprehensive look at the coaching process, the coach, the client, the supervisor and the relationships therein. The seven eyes are:
  - The client
  - The coaching process between coach and client
  - The relationship between the client and coach
  - The coach
  - The relationship between coach and supervisor
  - The coaching supervisor
  - The organisational context or system in which they all operate including professional codes and ethics, social context and norms, and organisational constraints.

- Using this model offers a lens on every aspect of coaching including the supervision process itself and relationship between coach and supervisor. In supervision sessions parallel processes can be played out as those between client and coach and when this is apparent for the coach, rich learning can come from the realisation and a new approach formulated to serve the client better.
- This model is also very helpful in viewing the coaching contract and its impact in the organisational context and is therefore a space to explore how coaching is viewed and its success in developing the organisation overall.

7.   Unconscious Processes

- If you are a coach, you will understand the unconscious processes that can occur between you and your clients. Having increased self-awareness about these unconscious processes in the coaching conversation helps to determine whether the issues discussed are our client's or our own and whether through the coaching process you may be for example, projecting your own emotions onto the client. Supervision raises this awareness of the psychological impact of coaching for the coach who can then take it back into their coaching practice.
- If you procure or manage coaching services internally or externally you need to ensure that your coaching providers engage with supervision to keep themselves and their clients safe in psychological terms. Recognition that supervision brings this self-awareness is key.

8.   Practicalities of Supervision Contracts

- As with any coaching contract, a contract for supervision will need to be clear in its aims and boundaries both for the coach and for you as the sponsor of such as contract.

115

You will need to identify with your supervisor(s) the number of sessions required, whether this is formal 1:1 supervision or group supervision and how those sessions are reported back to you as the sponsor.

- You will need to agree a level of confidentiality with the supervisor and the coaches that they supervise that does not put the supervisor/coach relationship under unnecessary pressure. That may only cover the reporting of whether the coach has attended supervision or not. Without the assurance that the conversation in the supervision session is confidential then the necessary rapport cannot be developed within that relationship just as in the coaching/client relationship.

- It can be useful sometimes to agree a limited report around emerging themes across the organisation rather than specific issues that may be attributable to individuals and thereby breaking boundaries on confidentiality. Whatever you decide to agree it needs to be transparent and open to both coaches, supervisors and staff who may be clients. Spend time in the planning and consultation phase of contracting to prevent problems arising later.

9.   Supervision = Growth

If you have already invested in coaching resources for your people whether internally provided or externally you have acknowledged that there is an intrinsic benefit to the organisation. Supervision is merely another investment to help your business/service grow and develop.

- By encouraging your coaches to engage with supervision you are empowering and enabling growth, through the offer of that supportive development.

- Bear in mind how your coaches are operating. Do they act as a change agent? Is it more for development? Is coaching employed to raise performance or to deal with a crisis?
  However, your coaching resource is employed you cannot expect a consistent high-quality result if the coaches themselves are left to support their own development.
- Development of your people through coaching and subsequently coaching supervision has the ability to close that feedback loop on organisational growth.

10. Development of coaching as a profession

- Peter Hawkins summarises this very well when he says *"Supervision needs to be a place of co-creative and generative thinking where new learning is being forged for the clients, coach, supervisor and the profession as a whole"*.
- See coaching supervision therefore as an opportunity to co-create a future for your business/organisation but moreover a place where new learning can emerge that will enrich the working lives of your people.
- The principle of supervision in coaching moves us towards a regulated profession where coaching can be recognised formally for its contribution to the health and wellbeing of our people in the same way as psychotherapy or other therapeutic interventions.

Further Reading – see end of book

YOUR NOTES FROM CHAPTER 9

Chapter 10

Top 10 Tips and Benefits of developing a longer term relationship with your Coaching Provider

By Dawn Scott

Potential clients often ask coaching providers how will coaching benefit our business? In today's world of instant gratification, it can be difficult to prove its worth in a matter of weeks. It often takes several sessions over some months before a break-through occurs with an individual client. It is in everyone's benefit therefore to develop a longer-term view of what coaching can do for your organisation.

So, ask yourself the question what will coaching do for my business and me? If the answer is that you want a quick fix then coaching is not the solution. The benefits of coaching are best seen over the longer term and this chapter highlights 10 key ways that a longer-term relationship with a coaching provider can offer for you your people and your business.

1.   Independent View

- An external provider is not part of your operational structure so not party to the internal politics or personal/team dynamics that play out day to day. The ability to remain objective is a key part of the coaching relationship and this reduces the likelihood for collusion in behaviour that inhibits growth.
- Objectivity where judgement is suspended both for the individual coaching client and the client organisation supports the integrity of the contract and the validity of the results.

2.   Feedback Loop

- With a longstanding relationship there is over time an ability to gather intelligence and monitor themes for your organisation. This may work as an early warning system about shifts in organisational culture or systemic issues that are problematic for the business.

- It is important to note that the coaching conversation is always confidential between coach and client but where the relationship between coaching provider and sponsor organisation is long term then themes do often emerge across the coaching contract as a whole.
- This intelligence can be shared with your board or management team for discussion of strategic impact and used as a staff engagement focus so that your people find their own solutions.
- Feedback can be provided in line with performance review systems where it relates to specific individuals or where systemic issues are affecting performance indicators.

3.   Trust & Confidence of Your People

- The coaching contract agreed between you and your coaching provider has at its heart confidentiality. Over time as people see this ethic upheld the trust and confidence in the coaching process grows; not only between coach and client but in the organisation's integrity to respect the process.
- There is sometimes suspicion that coaching masks another management agenda and therefore the long-term relationship can demonstrate much more clearly that this is not the case. If your people trust the process they are more likely to accept and work for mutually beneficial outcomes.

4.   Critical Friend

- The coach's role is to sit alongside a client and ask questions; provide another perspective. Where a coach provider is able to develop this over time they get to know you and your business very well.
- Understanding the context in which you and your people operate provides a much richer picture for the coaching itself and this will help the coach to

prompt or question their clients with added confidence.

- The development of this role as critical friend offers the business an important perspective when group think takes over or to challenge you to think differently in good times and in bad.

5.   Partnership for improvement

"At no time in history have we needed such system leaders more. We face a host of systemic challenges beyond the reach of existing institutions and their hierarchical authority structures. Problems like climate change, destruction of ecosystems, growing scarcity of water, youth unemployment, and embedded poverty and inequity require unprecedented collaboration among different organizations, sectors, and even countries. Sensing this need, countless collaborative initiatives have arisen in the past decade— locally, regionally, and even globally. Yet more often than not they have floundered—in part because they failed to foster collective leadership within and across the collaborating organizations"

Senge, Hamilton & Kania 2015 *The Dawn of System Leadership** Standford Social Innovation Review Standford University * https://ssir.org/articles/entry/the_dawn_of_system_leadership

- More and more businesses are being asked to work outside of their traditional boundaries to meet what are often global challenges in the market place.   The system in which you operate continually has to shift and adapt to meet clients needs.   Working in partnership with a range of providers and suppliers of goods and services is part of the system in which you operate. Developing a collective approach to problem solving to improve performance in this environment is a necessity for success.

122

- See your coach provider as an integral part of that system and make it an explicit part of the coaching contract that your relationship is key for the long-term development of the organisation.

6.   The wider network

- Bringing in external coaching resource is a connection to a wide network of expertise and learning that would otherwise be absent from your team.
- The long-term benefit of this is that the network grows, extending beyond the coaching relationship and bringing access to a continual supply of fresh knowledge to your organisation.
- Your coach provider will in turn have a network, which you can tap into that can reap considerable benefits. One NHS client we have worked with was challenged with funding available to continue with the leadership programme we had developed and delivered with them. Our Project Director of the Programme had in her network a contact at the local authority that she knew to have a substantial in-house coaching resource. Following a phone call and meeting to discuss the opportunities for partnership on the programme we were able to secure 8 experienced coaches for the next programme at no extra investment but as a goodwill gesture to support partnership working across the public sector.

7.   Measuring Return on Investment

- Every coaching contract sets out clear aims for achievement with the individual client and in a three-way contract builds in expectations of the sponsor organisation or business which may look at the return on investment.

- The impact of coaching often takes a number of months and years (in the case of a coaching culture – see the section on shaping culture) and therefore longer-term goals can be set and tested fully to realise the benefits. If you wanted to reduce staff turnover for example, as a quantifiable outcome of coaching support this can be measured before and after coaching interventions for individuals and teams. Where locum or interim cover is purchased to cover vacancies then this can be seen as a direct saving to the business.
- The real impact of coaching can be quantified in longer term for example with the measurement of performance improvement both for individual performance and overall delivery of business targets say through a sales team who may have been underachieving.

8. Talent Management

- Talent management is the lifeblood of any organisation. If you don't offer your talent support and development i.e. they don't see a future for themselves, all your best people will flow out of the door. Support for your people through coaching provides a clear message to those aspiring individuals that they are valued through your investment in them.
- A coach can identify new talent and then work alongside them and the business to develop those individuals over the longer term, through 3-way contracts developed with Line Management that support the achievement of business objectives.

9. Changing Behaviour

- We often work with organisations in regulated industries where performance outcomes are measured and made public. Where performance is deteriorating, coaching of teams and individuals

124

across Executive, Senior and Middle Management delivers real behaviour change that can make the difference between good and excellent performance or survival when at risk of disqualification and loss of accreditation to operate.

- Changing the behaviour of your people to meet these challenges is a longer- term expectation and therefore developing a longer-term relationship with your coach provider in these circumstances enables clear outcomes to be set and realised in a more realistic timeframe.

10. Shaping the culture

- Shaping the culture of your organisation can only be realised over the longer term - take the McKinsey 7 S Model illustrated below; coaching is often employed to develop the "softer" elements of the model so Skills, Staff, Style and Shared Values. However coaching is often a great approach through team coaching or problem solving to develop the "Harder" elements of Strategy Structure and Systems.
- It is vital therefore for a longer term coaching strategy to be developed alongside other enabling measures in your Organisation Development Plan that will shape the culture and deliver the success you are aiming for.

Figure 1: The McKinsey 7S Model

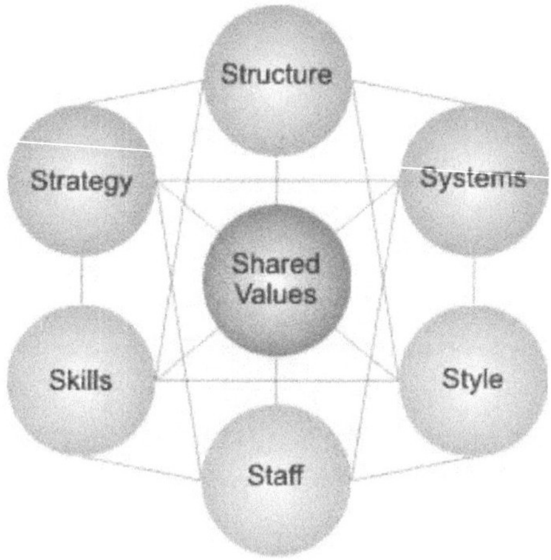

Conclusions

It is therefore an essential part of your organisation's development plan to form long-term relationships with your coaching provider. Make sure that you recruit a provider that shares your business values and is one that you can trust and work alongside. Test out the service on offer and dig deep to understand the true ethos that drives their business. Once aligned, those values and motivation to drive progress will ultimately benefit all those in the partnership.

YOUR NOTES FROM CHAPTER 10

LEARNING ZONE

Welcome to the Learning Zone!

Here you will find some tools that are mentioned in the book.

You can freely access blank master forms by visiting http://100TopTips.com

Click on "Learning Zone Forms"

You will have to create a username and password to access the forms.

Please be assured that your information will NOT be passed to a third party and we fully comply with GDPR regulations.

The forms available from this book are;

Basic Coaching Agreement

Quarterly Coaching Action Plan

Basic Coaching Agreement Page 1

Coaching Agreement

Organisation:				
Client:	Name:		Title:	
Line Manager/Sponsor:	Name:		Title:	
HR Sponsor:	Name:		Title:	
Coach:	Primary:		Start date:	
Programme Scope:	No. of sessions:	Frequency:		Session length: hrs/mins
Specific Tools/diagnostics:				

1. **CURRENT SITUATION:**
   What is the business need? What led to this coaching programme?

Copyright of Ian Munro 2012 onwards

Coaching Agreement

2. **DEVELOPMENT AREAS:**
   Identify 2-3 key development needs or opportunities and their associated business impact

GOAL 1

GOAL 2

GOAL 3

3. **DESIRED RESULTS:**
   What different behaviours/results will be apparent? How will the desired results impact the business?

GOAL 1

GOAL 2

GOAL 3

Sponsor signature: _____ (optional)

Copyright of Ian Munro 2012 onwards

Basic Coaching Agreement Page 2

Coaching Agreement

4. **MEASUREMENT:**
   When and who will engage in programme reviews/measures?

   Rate on a scale of 1 – 10, where 1 is low and 10 is high. How else will progress be measured?

GOAL 1

Rating on commencement of programme ☐   Rating on completion of programme ☐

Other Measures:

GOAL 2

Rating on commencement of programme ☐   Rating on completion of programme ☐

Other Measures:

GOAL 3

Rating on commencement of programme ☐   Rating on completion of programme ☐

Other Measures:

Reviewer _____

Copyright of Ian Munro 2012 onwards

Coaching Agreement

5. **COACHING FEEDBACK :**
   This organisation continually strives to improve the quality of their coaching. Sharing with your coach feedback to the following questions will help to continue this process:

   - What worked particularly well in your coaching programme?

   - What could have been even better?

   - What did you achieve as a result of the coaching?

   - What was your overall experience of this coaching programme?

Copyright of Ian Munro 2012 onwards

Quarterly Coaching Action Plan

QUARTERLY COACHING ACTION PLAN

Quarter   /Year

List your Goals and Development Areas for the current quarter, followed by the tasks for each one. As the quarter progresses complete the outcome box. Start the process again at the following quarter.

GOALS, DEVELOPMENT AREAS	TASKS FOR QUARTER	OUTCOME	NOTES
1.	1.1 1.2 1.3 1.4	1.1 1.2 1.3 1.4	
2	2.1 2.2 2.3 2.4	2.1 2.2 2.3 2.4	
3	3.1 3.2 3.3 3.4	3.1 3.2 3.3 3.4	
4	4.1 4.2 4.3 4.4	4.1 4.2 4.3 4.4	
5	5.1 5.2 5.3 5.4	5.1 5.2 5.3 5.4	
6	6.1 6.2 6.3 6.4	6.1 6.2 6.3 6.4	

© Ian Munro 2013 onwards

Summary

We hope that you will have found this book of real benefit.

As stated in the Introduction we have tried to make this a clear guide about how the Coaching world works.

Feedback from readers helps us to further fine tune our material, so please keep the emails coming to:

feedback.coaching@100toptips.com

Our best wishes to you all.

The Authors

About the Authors

Bob Baker has worked for over twenty years in development and academic programmes. He has a 15 years successful track record in leadership development and coaching including tutoring on post-graduate programmes. Bob has particular interest in improving coaching quality and the role of supervision.

Dawn Scott served 5 years at Board level both as CEO and Director in the NHS. A qualified Executive Coach for 10 years, Dawn enjoys working with Corporate Leaders, Executive Managers, Business Owners & Clinicians to explore a fresh perspective on career, life, relationship and personal development issues

Ian Munro is the founder of the 100 Top Tips book project. He is also an active executive coach working across the private and public sectors. Coaching for over 20 years Ian works to develop people in their workplace and take ownership of their careers. He is also a director of several companies.

Mark Greenfield has over twenty-five years coaching experience in the private, public and voluntary sectors. He has an interest in top team coaching, working with Boards and Executive teams to improve their trust, cohesion and results. Mark coaches senior leaders through challenging times in their careers.

Melanie Warner is a business psychologist and coach, passionate about people development. She has extensive experience in the learning and development profession. Melanie has worked as an organisational development consultant with major organisations in the private and public sectors

Mike Nelson is an organisation consultant with specific expertise in coaching and leadership development. With a background in UK Healthcare and a national UK retailer he works across all sectors. Mike has operated for several years as an Organisational Consultant and Executive Coach.

Vicky Glanville is a coach, marketing consultant and yoga teacher. She is a passionate portfolio careerist and loves to combine all 3! Coaching for over 8 years, she was part of The AA's coaching team. As a marketing specialist of more than 20 years, she advises Healthskills and other organisations about all things marketing.

Some of the other Authors we mention

Loganbill C Hardy \E & Delworth U (1982) *Supervision a conceptual model* The counselling Psychologist 10:1 3-42

Proctor B (1988a) *Supervision a working alliance* (videotape training manual) St Leonards-on-sea Alexia Productions

Hawkins P Shohet R (2000) *Supervision in the Helping Professions* McGraw Hill OU Press

Hawkins P (2012) *Creating a Coaching Culture* McGraw Hill OU Press

What works in Coaching de Haan 2016 www.trainingjournal.com

7 Habits of Highly Effective People – Steven Covey – Simon & Shuster 1992

Myers-Briggs Foundation – MBTI

Firo B Shutz W.C. and Firo A 3 Dimensional Theory of Interpersonal Behaviour

Leadership Practices Inventory – B Posner & Kouzes – Pfeiffer 2003

The 5 Dysfunctions of a Team – Patrick Lencioni – Jossey/Bass – 2002

Overcoming the Five Dysfunctions of a Team: A Field Guide – Jossey-Bass – Lencioni, P. - 2005

The International Journal of Mentoring and Coaching Volume V Issue 1, 03/2007

Carter and Connage 2007

Putting Learning Styles to work – Alan Mumford – Action Learning at work – Gower - 1997

The one-minute Manager – Blanchard & Johnson – Fontana/Collins – 1983

The Wisdom of Teams: Creating the High Performance Organisation – Harvard Business School Press – Katzenbach, J. & Smith, D. - 2005

Leadership Team Coaching - Kogan Page – Hawkins, P. – 2011

The Leadership Challenge: the Five Practices of Exemplary Leadership – Jossey-Bass – Kouzes, J. & Posner, B. – 2002

Supervision a conceptual model - The Counselling Psychologist 10:1 3-42 - Loganbill C Hardy E & Delworth U - 1982

Supervision a working alliance (videotape training manual) - St Leonards-on-sea Alexia Productions - Proctor B - 1988a

Supervision in the Helping Professions - McGraw Hill OU Press - Hawkins P Shohet R - 2000

Creating a Coaching Culture - McGraw Hill OU Press - Hawkins P - 2012

The Coaching Manual: The definitive guide to the process, principles and skills of personal coaching. Julie Starr. 4th Edition 2016

Coaching for Performance: The principles and practice of coaching and leadership. Sir John Whitmore. 5th Edition2017

THIS FINAL PAGE IS FOR YOUR LAST NOTES!

Here is a final tip. If you lend this book to someone, put their name and the date you lent it on this page. This may improve your chances of getting it back!

BV - #0024 - 050219 - C0 - 234/156/9 - PB - 9780993465871